A Biplane Book

Alone...
by
Rod McKuen

PUBLISHED BY POCKET BOOKS PRINTED IN U.S.A.

A Biplane Book

ALONE

POCKET BOOK edition published June, 1975

In addition to the books listed on the Sources page, some of the poems in this collection have appeared in *The New York Times, Folio, Woman's Day, Saturday Review,* and *The Christian Science Monitor*.

L

Standard Book Number 671–80020–5.

Cover and art direction by Hy Fujita.

Photography by Hy Fujita, Rod McKuen, Donald Bradburn, David Nutter, Jim Marshall, Dor Neukcum, Herb Ball.

Coordinator for POCKET BOOKS: Jonathon Brodman.

265

Printed in the U.S.A.

For further information, please contact Cheval/Stanyan Co., 8440 Santa Monica Blvd., Los Angeles, California 90069.

This book is for
those people who never knew,
and those who did.

Books by Rod McKuen

Poetry
And Autumn Came
Stanyan Street & Other Sorrows
Listen to the Warm
Lonesome Cities
In Someone's Shadow
Caught in the Quiet
Fields of Wonder
And to Each Season
Come to Me in Silence
Moment to Moment
Beyond the Boardwalk

Collected Poems
Twelve Years of Christmas
With Love . . .
The Carols of Christmas
Seasons in the Sun
Alone

Collected Lyrics
New Ballads
Pastorale
The Songs of Rod McKuen
Grand Tour

Song Books
The Annotated Rod McKuen Song Book

Foreword

What follows in this book is a collection of poetry and prose that touches on a number of subjects; they have, however, the umbrella—I might have said electric blanket—of being written of and about the state of *alone*.

Attempting to define *alone* is futile; the symptoms and the end result are always different. It is enough to say that if you believe yourself to be alone, you are. Seemingly, there is almost no way to set about with any success to circumvent or avoid its coming—even as you see it approaching in the distance. But most often *alone* can be reasoned with and it passes. Someone comes by and makes it pass. If not, take it as a partner. We've all known worse.

Alone is not the end—or it shouldn't be. In truth, it is a starting place. One more square one for reaching out.

I am not a joiner. Somewhere I once said that people join clubs now for the very reason they once carried them, a need for security. Maybe I'm alone more often than I should be, because I try to find security within myself.

Though I believe very strongly in social intercourse, mentally and otherwise, the man who detailed the advantages of masturbation as not having to dress up, being certain not to disappoint anyone, done on your own time and at your appointed place, and, best of all, meeting a better class of people, did have a point of view hardly arguable.

Alone, like love, regardless of what the primers say, can be a noun, pronoun, adverb, or adjective—depending on its use and the extent to which it comes, stays, or returns to your life. Darkness and retreat have more than once been my cover. By now I've traveled deep enough into the darkness that hiking back through any clearing is a journey not taken without some thought.

With growing frequency I now plan nightly outings in the morning, await them through the day, and with approaching darkness work myself into an apathy that a closing battle line could not penetrate. I am never sure what I miss by staying home. Doubtlessly, I've avoided disappointments that might have chipped away a little more of my self-confidence. Possibly on one given night I missed the silver apple that, bitten into, would have changed my life.

I chose the shadows; they did not choose me. I stay here securely not just because I feel plain, but because disappearance is by now the easy way. The habit. The worn path that I can trod knowingly and be assured safe passage home.

Don't ask me how it might have been, or what it could or should have been like. How different all my days would be if I'd strode securely into public sunlight. More and more I take the sun alone—always at the edge of the clearing, close enough to the wood to crouch low or retreat at ease should the beautiful enemy pass by.

I have never said I liked always being alone. I have said I like it better than being with *just anybody.* The need to merely touch someone I've seen, or imagined, can be so great at times that it's as close to madness as I ever hope to come.

The brushing of two minds, or hands, or bodies together. Even eyes focused at distance can make the loneliest of us all alive and full of hope—momentary or otherwise. And I have known two minds and bodies seemingly compatible in every way to meet in love and be so alone together you would swear they'd never met. We do meet each other over and over every day. But centuries can seemingly go by before two people meet in some special way that causes an end to their individual loneliness.

Much of this book is new. Since I go on being the same man trying to find the answers to some of the same questions, some of these poems will be newer to me than they are to you. Other poems were written years ago, but never shown or shared, and some are taken from other collections. If I have to describe them, *personal* and *private* come to mind. But those words, too, have been for me nouns, pronouns, verbs—far more than adjectives.

If these pages are so *personal* and *private*, why

let them go? Why not? There is a chance, however small, that some *one* will read, understand, even stop and turn in my direction.

To repeat myself, sometimes someone passes by and stops; then you're not alone. Some of these words are smoke signals.

Rod McKuen—1975

Publisher's Note

This is only the second collection of poetry and prose published in paperback by Rod McKuen. Originally intended as collections drawn from his earlier works, each has turned into a literary work of its own. Despite the inclusion of many of the author's best-loved poems, there is enough new material in this book for a volume all by itself.

Seasons in the Sun, while meant to be a series of Mr. McKuen's poems using the summer season as a canvas, has been read and reread as an independent work and praised by critics and the public alike.

The "Sources" section at the end of the book detailing the origin of each poem in **ALONE** is complete and informative. Both publisher and author request that you turn to it only after a first reading of the complete text.

Contents

for Sarah Churchill

Solitaire

Solitaire

The stone cries out. A whisper first, a moan
and then a muffled shout. Nobody listens.
Why bother with the stone, the single singing
rock, the lone man dealing out the cards upon
the table in the game of solitaire?
   The soloist, whether up above the orchestra,
on the outside of the woods beyond the meatrack
or in the farthest elbow of a crowded room, is asking
to be left alone or crying out for company.
No matter. Very rarely does the solo player
engage in double solitaire. The reason is a
simple one—always there's a chance of winning.

Oval Window

There is
an oval window
in my bathroom
at Très Vidas
surrounded by some vines.
Each evening—or almost—
a single *geko* comes
attracted to the light
where he hangs
against the pane
        till morning.

Being on the inside
I see his underside
beautiful, motionless
                    and white

I wish we had
a meeting language.
I want to know
            about him.
He seems so solitary,
                    unafraid.
I am attracted
to solitary things.

Lesson: Two

Standing still
behind the window
cut off from the traffic
and the truth by glass.

I do not live
       within a lie
because I do not
       live at all.
Perhaps I've found
a kind of purgatory
just before the truth
but if it waits beyond
it's out of sight.

High Heavens There Are

High heavens there are
low heavens too
and as many in between
as there are clouds
to populate the ones
                  we know.

I watch. I wait.
Not for any paths
        to open up
that point to heavens
             near or far,
but for something.

Something
isn't always very much
but more often than not
something's more than nothing.

August 31

they're binding up
the book on august now
placing it in exile
making way for another
proud september coronation.

lines scribbled
on the pages of a diary
a date on the calendar
                    circled
a faded tan
a forgotten man
and august dies.

Thursday Evening

Good-bye.
I know no other way
    to say it.
What shall I call you?
       Never mind.
This poem is for you
and you will know it
in Munich or in Minnesota.

It only complicates
my life as well as yours
to set your name down here
as well as detail
inch by inch the night.

The windmills turn
and we turn, too,
not with the wind
but slowly
imperceptibly away.

Not noticed by the sunset—
        if there is one
or by anyone.
Not we ourselves.

We will not walk again
along canals together.
And the record player
will not play *We Will*.

It's somehow
        miracle enough
that Amstel beer in
            Amsterdam
made us drunk enough
to meet at all.

Still, September has
        a way with it
and a way of coming round
next year
        and the next year, too.

And Thursday comes around
at least once every week.

Paris

I've drawn your face
on tablecloths
across the country.
Tracing your smile
with my index finger,
making your hair just so.
Till now you're more
what I want you to be
than what you are.

I can paint your eyes
                    and say
there is where I lived
for twenty minutes
            and more.

I order grapefruit
and pay for ruined napkins.
And between the morning
                    and the evening
I draw your face
a little fainter every day.

Shadows and Safety

Mr. Kelly barks
      at shadows now;
   that's a habit
that he'll have to break.
For shadows offer
all the safety left in life.

I dare not think
what might replace
          the shadows
that I've had to learn
          to love.

I stand ready yet again
to learn a new geography
if that becomes
a necessary thing to do.
Meanwhile
there's a certain sureness
in the dark parts of the house.
for you're still hiding there. .

Oakland Bus Depot/1951

alone in the busy station
                    I waited
but you never arrived.
people came and went
little family pageants
                    were enacted
over and over again
and still
you did not come.

I watched
the wall clock
picked out
        the dispatcher's
every scrambled word
I waited
and the hour grew late
still no you.

and so very weary
I left the station
and went home.

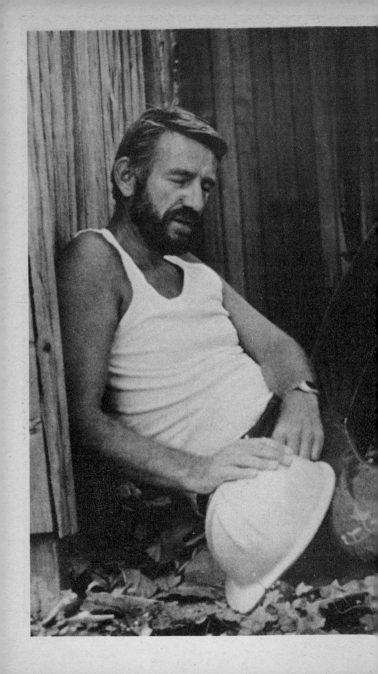

for Dusty Springfield

The Spectator

The Spectator

My religion is well known to those few who know me. I believe in bodies, arms entangling and untangling. I believe, and I know it to be so, that there are so many curves and hollows in a single body that none of us can come to know them all within a single lifetime.

I believe in one to one and one on one. No wine or magic, no hand-me-down Bible can improve on that.

I believe in spring, but only if I'm rolled up in a pillow or holding some well-loved face in my hands or my imagination is any world green enough for me.

More often I'm a spectator, meaning I've no reason to believe in anything save what I see. But I do. I know there is more to seeing than looking, but I go on looking.

Journeymen

Life goes slow without love.
It moves along unhurried.
The sun rises.
        The sun goes down.

There are those who pass by
changing the time-cycle
if you're willing to wait.

I am always shy
with these journeymen
              at first
and by the time
        I get to know them
they've gone away.

Holidays

Holidays were made
for lonely people.
I always meet
the best of these
when holidays are near.
                            Rented rooms
become the place to go,
        not fireworks
                or carnivals
                        or musical parades,
but rented rooms
        with granite basins
and people
who forget your name
before you finish
going down the stairs.

Holidays mean the most
when you're celebrating
what you've found yourself.

Love is a season
and holidays like signposts
mark the time.

Jimjann

I wanted you
that day at the beach
because you were beautiful
because you smiled
and because I knew
your world was different.

But I lost you
even before we met
and I ran on the beach all day
to relieve the tension.

Better to live
in a birdless country
                    without sun
than go your way alone—
                    always.
But what could I have said?
Your smile was a warm wall.

Room

Ceiling cracks,
    dusty woodwork,
a spider's web half started,
I know this room by heart.
I find my way
from bed to toilet
in the middle of
    the darkest night.

Half asleep or wide awake
I need no map
to help me thread my way
past and in between
the obstacles that fill up full
    this empty room.

I'd post a letter
but I don't know
        your address.
I'd call
but how would I begin
let alone maintain
        a conversation?
Once I'd promised
to forget you
I ran backward
        making sure
that I'd remember you
for always.

The doorbell buzzes
at odd times
in the morning
          or the night,
maybe all day long
if I were here
  to hear it.

I never answer,
since it isn't you.
And if it were
on opening the door
I'd only open
brand new memories
that even as they happened
I'd be making resolutions
          to forget.

State Beach

He turned
and moved to go
        into the water
she followed close behind.
The sun caught
        the color of her hair
and the bronze of his legs
and I caught them both
held them in my gaze
till they were
        out of sight
splashing in the sun
lost in the waves.

I think
I have never been in love
                more than now
here on a native beach
watching other lovers
do familiar things
and make familiar love.
I think I have never
missed you more.

And as the last October sun
goes beyond the ocean
        to its resting place
and the umbrellas are folded
the rumpled pants
        and rumpled dresses
slipped over
        the wet bathing suits,
the sound of a Tokyo spring
echoes in my ears
I walk with you
            down
                dark
                    streets
and the rain
comes down like tears.

Video Tape

I let go. I do.
You should see me
in the middle night
moving in on strangers
for the kill
　　　or the caress,
admonishing
to the newfound friend
my version of
　　　the kiss of life.

You should view
the front part of my head
as it calls back you
while I'm using
all those bodies new
and never seen again.

Tuesday Afternoon

A cat
came off the higher roof
and down below my window
balancing on so thin a rail
that even pigeons had not dared
that tightrope walk before.

A red and yellow cat
          of some age
and some experience
sat the afternoon out
down below my window—waiting
as he must have known
    I waited.

A cat for company
until the sunset started
then he leisurely climbed back.

for Phyllis Wilkie

Encounters

By Their Numbers You Will Know Them

Encounters are the footsteps up and down the ladder or through the littered alleyways of time. As such, not to be taken lightly, or cherished beyond their reality as food for the imagination's future. A friend once told me that to every new encounter he gave only what he himself needed in return.

Fifteen years later I still see him backed up against the jukebox in the same bar where we met before. He looks unchanged, still wearing the old school tie (though the school itself's been razed), still posturing as though a sculptor chiseled him into that single pose and welded him forever there. He even says the same things to me as I pause, nod hello, and then pass over to the next bar continuing in the hunt.

What he says mostly is, "Don't let anyone come too close to you." I smile and nod, because I know that he expects me to smile and nod in silent agreement.

My friend looks the same as fifteen years ago, except when you get close.

While Drifting

This is the way it was
while I was waiting
for your eyes to find me.

I was drifting
          going no place.
Hypnotized by sunshine
                    maybe,
barking back at seals
along the beach.

Skipping flat stones
          on the water,
but much too wise
          for sand castles.
My castles were
          across the sea
or still within my mind.

There were the beach bars
and the other beach people
sometimes little bedrooms
          were my beach,
     but I was drifting.

I must have thought
the night could save me
and I went down
            into pillows
looked up through
            dirty windows
smiled back from
            broken mattresses
turned in Thunderbirds
and kissed in elevators.

I cried too sometimes.
            For me.

I loved every face
I thought looked pretty
and every kindred eye
I caught in crowds.
            But I was drifting,
            before you.

Advance/Retreat

No woman held a man
the way that you
hold onto me just now,
or if one did
I never heard about it
not in a story book
        or at my ear.

If it were so,
if there were even *one*
one experience the same as this
on record or on file,
surely I would know.
Surely I would hear
the celebrating
      down the street
as someone else found out
just how it is to be Columbus
for the length of time
             you're here.

School

Before the Palmer method
taught me how
to write my name,
I'd learned to read *love*
in the salesman's face.

And so
without the aid
of Dick and Jane,
by myself I've come
unadorned and plain
to offer you
      without condition
a life just past
and just beginning.

Soldier, One/Tagu, Korea—1955

The tall soldier's helmet
gleaming in the sun
he stands apart a little
        from the rest,
a vanguard
in the narrow street
between the rows
of yellow barracks.

Passing past each other
our eyes meet in challenge,
or is it recognition?

Were you expecting?
I must admit
        I half expected you,
though I could not divine
the time of day
        you might arrive,
I perceived your coming.
And I surmise
that I was waiting.

                Now?
Truce perhaps
and only later trust.
And if later never comes
there was that instant
of challenge or concern.

I will always choose
to think of it
        as recognition.

The Hermit Crab

As I watch you
move beyond the door
I remember
          that some oceans
have been known
          to come again
to their mother country
and wash ashore
more brilliant
               treasures
than they took away.

It is small comfort
to a man who lately
greets each season
as the hermit crab,
hiding in the rocks
and scurrying
          from intruders
be they from the land
                    or sea.

On the Way to Sacramento

The three of us
on our way to Sacramento
and no one speaking.
Each having committed
the error of caring
          for the other—
                but separately.

And all the while
we thought we were different.
From what, I wonder?
Passion doesn't even need
                    the wind,
it is a need unto itself.

Where friendship lurked
and love once lived
now only silence dwells
and truth between us
will not come again.

Now we're altogether naked,
even to the autumn trees,
and yet more private
than we'll ever be.

I wish that I were home
wherever home is now.
Instead of being only
one more passenger of hate
on this third day of October
riding down the California
                    highway.
I wish that I were home
                for always.

I pray that I might never be
amazed and let down
          even once again
by those I trust.

Not possible? I know.
Then I pray
we'll all reach Sacramento
                    soon.

The Need (Thirty-six)

It's nice sometimes
to open up the heart a little
and let some hurt come in.
It proves you're still alive.

If nothing else
it says to you—
clear as high hill air,
              uncomfortable
as diving through
              cold water—

I'm here.
However wretchedly I feel,
                I feel.

I'm not sure
why we cannot shake
the old loves
        from our minds.
It must be that
we build on memory
and make them more
        than what they were.
And is the manufacture
just a safe device
for closing up the wall?

I do remember.
The only fuzzy circumstance
is sometimes where and how.
Why, I know.

It happens
        just because we need
to want and to be
                wanted, too,
when love is here or gone
to lie down in the darkness
and listen to the warm.

Poem

The smell goes first.
          The smell
that closed rooms have
when women are about.

No coffee smell,
no sweet stale smell
          of bath,
no hair smell
      on the pillow,
no smell of beds
too long unchanged.

I kept the window
closed all day
trying to retain
what little of you
there was left.

And now the darkness
        like firecrackers
ringing in my ears,
trying to sleep
in that same unchanged bed
calling back old images
to make the evening
        come out right.

Supper

All hills and gullies
mounds and little mountains
you rise up early
      in the night
In dreams so real
that sleep and waking
meet, dissolve and blur.

A sacrament you are
         made of salt
and tasting not unlike
cinnamon or soda water
as I pull you to me.

A meal you are.
A meal you make of me.

We devour
one the other
as though we were
some hungry giants
having fasted
all the winter
hungry now for spring.

I see no end
to this stored-up appetite
        this emptiness
that only loving
up and down a lifetime
        will fill up.

I have wished too much
or just enough
          to bring you here
almost to the final step.

One meter gone
or one mile away
               you are
just out of reach
or too near
to make perspective work.

for Frank Sinatra

Night Crawler

Night

I can just about get through the day, but the night makes me nervous. Not for any reason except maybe that it catches you *unaware*, and follows you the way a woman does when she wants something.

I've been in every kind of night so I shouldn't be afraid of darkness. But for some reason the night makes me nervous.

April 12

We come into the world
                      alone.
We go away the same.
We're meant to spend
the interlude between
                in closeness
or so we tell ourselves.
But it's a long way
from the morning
       to the evening.

Day Song

The freckled morning
moving into day now,
I stand at the window
    half dressed,
watching the snow melt
as quickly as it falls.

A hundred blank windows
in the building now going up
    across the street
look back at me.
My expression is as empty
    as theirs,
as the long slow business
of learning how
    to live alone
        begins again.

Night Song

The shadowed afternoon
moving into night now,
I close the door behind me
and hurry down the stairs.

Saturday night
is better than Friday.
If you don't make out
you can always take home
*the great American
consolation prize*,
thirty cents' worth of love,
  the Sunday paper.

Hotel Room

The hotel room
is four flights up
just high enough
for me to see
the tops of heads
I'll never touch.
Brown hair,
         yellow hair,
hatless heads
and heads with hats.
People alone,
         people together
watched
    by my sniper's eye,
poised to drop
invisible love bombs.

Poem, 2

I have no special bed.
I give myself to those
　　　　　who offer love.
Can it be wrong?
Lonely rivers
　　　　going to the sea
　　give themselves
to many brooks in passing.

So it is with me
undiscovered and alone
till someone says
　　　　the magic word,
　　　　　　hello.

You'll see me then
some weekend waiting
and if you do
　　　　say hello.

Winter Night

For the quiet
that you've brought
              into my life,
the stillness
when you're here,
I bow to you
and bend you over
as my final love.

Final? Yes.
And I've no doubt
that as
        the drowned man
washed up
on the shore,
one day I'll be
beached as well.
To that direction
            I move then,
unafraid.
Assuming I'll have
yet another quiet night
            with you.

Those Who Found the Time

My vision
of a lilac world
is held in trust for me
by friends
   who'll never know
         they're friends.
And lovers I've held
      only once.

I'd let them know, but how?
I'd fit them in, but when?
Still no one's needs
   are that of being
       fitted in.

Every man demands
his full round
share of time.

But on those few
who've found the time
        to fit me in,
schedule me somehow
within their crowded lives.
They are remembered
        almost daily.
                At night
each of them returns
every bit as real
as lilac smells
        on April days.

The Dandelion

The dandelion
hasn't yet been known
to make a choice
between the pasture
        and the lawn
and love's as blind
        to rank or right
as politicians
are to pulse beats.

Only desperation
cuts through everything.

Know that
I'm a desperate man
when in your arms,
more so when you're away.

I wind my watch
when it needs no winding.
I puzzle harder puzzles
than my mind
            can comprehend.
By these simple acts
I manage for a time
to ward off facing
yet another
      confrontation
with your absence.

How is it
that I've come to this
unable once again
          to fill up
even one more day
          alone?

Concerto for Four Hands

Those waiting shadows
have always come along
in time to save me
from the mischief
            of myself.
Now in this
        snow-baroque winter
this Telemann time
                of Empty
do some shadows
            not yet formed
conspire to fill
        my empty mattress,
my too-wide room?

Come soon then
for I am growing tired
                of Telemann
I could use some Bach.

I Roll Better with the Night

Wrestling
with the morning,
I come out the loser.

Lying on the mat
looking up between
the thighs of yesterdays,
I imagine myself
    being elevated,
          picked up,
held—not let go.

Friendly arms around me
Firm friendly hands
        slipping slowly
into my back pockets,
pressing hard and holding me.
Then one hand spreading
in a catlike move
across my back—
hands becoming arms
arms becoming all
      and everything.

I roll better
       with the night.
I come up easy
falling back
only when I'm tired
     and happy.

April Man
for my brothers
Edward and Bill

An April evening
tangled in the river's tail
whining of itself
as the wind does
in the eaves
      of broken buildings.

Crickets—
    If they are crickets
sound like sea gulls
      or the crackling fire
as every bit of life there is
is trapped above the river
        or below.

I am not signaling
for May to come
nor tapping out
          a message
to the ears of June.
I'm held in place
and helpless,
like a given April night
the tail
      of some brown river
still holds onto.

I've brought you
nothing new
nor can I lead you
through tomorrow.
But if you travel back
to where I am
I'll let you stroke the tail
of my brown river
or wrap your naked limbs
around your battered brother
who has given in
but still remains
an April man.

for Dick Joslyn

The Loner

Sheridan Square, '74/A Diary in Miniature

November 1. Coming cross-country taking separate routes but traveling in a parallel direction. First connected by a leaflet passed from your hand into mine, eyes engaged for seconds only.

I thought nothing of that meeting, or whatever, if anything, might come later. Besides, we only smiled, backtracked, spoke in double paragraphs, smiled again and moved apart.

November 2. I came, and afterward came back. Here we are. Talking at your eight-o'clock-till-ten-o'clock, except on matinee days, door. I am quiet, show respect. There are truer words for that—overwhelmed, afraid, polite. We talk. Has *nothing* ever been said so badly? The vital minute passes. I hesitate, then leave. Outside in the car I stammer, stumble over words. My friends smile. They understand. I pretend to them I don't. Christ, it's happening again. And I am letting it happen.

Four A.M. Sylvia Syms has finished all her dead-end songs and I'm dead-ended.

November 3. I missed my plane. I will never know if it was done deliberately. London is put off another day. A reprieve. I come into the night to see you. No luck. I leave instructions where I'll be. An option; you can call tomorrow.

I wait. I over-wait. You do not come. I am elated. I am relieved. I am depressed. The jukebox owes me fifty quarters. I owe my friends a better smile. I put it on, go out into the cold. Back to the hotel. I watch a television movie, believe it or not, *Secret of the Incas* with Yma Sumac. Surely you will call me up tomorrow. The tub's filling up. I strip off my clothes. Think. Fuck thinking.

November 4. Up noon. Breakfast. I write. I'm finishing a book, this book. The phone rings with twenty-minute precision, every twenty minutes. Three-thirty now. I run through the options: no message was delivered; the signals passed between us were imagined by me; you occupy another man's bed; you are afraid. No, you are not afraid. You will not call.

Five. Darkness soon. London will not wait again. Anyway, what possible new excuses could I make, even to myself?

With no more knowledge of each other than a half-imagined look, I miss you mightily. You have caused a void that you will likely never hear about. Worse, I've occupied these hours we might have spent together writing of the time as substitute for not living it.

I remember California. I know you thought that I'd forgotten. What I did forget is that people seldom change their minds. Much as I dislike good-byes, I hate indifference more. Still, you were special. Waiting tables, filling up a stage, sliding through a Friday night in Sheridan Square, you were the prize. The mirrored ball spinning through the air, that once lit up, sends flecks of light dancing, bouncing, all across the discothèque. What I really thought was this—maybe you'd forgotten California and me. Maybe I'd be new to you, as you thought you were to me.

New York in November, the event of the season for some. For others, the pageantry and hope would have to be enough. Though it would not, could not be for me.

Closet

It is a fact
and not a pun
        that some
huff and hoist barbells
to attract bar belles.

Some work out
to keep from
going out and working.

Some spend their lives
in gyms around the world
afraid to face the fact
that what they really want
is one, two,
        maybe three
trips around the world
with Joe or Jack or Jim.

Kearny Street

The house
on Kearny Street
where I came and went
        on weekends
            is the same.
The hill above
      is summer green
the sky a foggy blue
and children still march by
each day at three o'clock
foraging back from school.
The hill and Kearny Street
are still the same
      but I have changed.

No more
the winning smile
the hasty song
the happy stare of love
the young heart
             leaping
      in the dark room.
And no more
the wild young man
who talked too quickly
      and too loud
of love he owned
and wished to give away.

Seldom the sun catches me
lying in bed late
                anymore.
Seldom the pigeons
gargling in the grass
see my form
stretched out upon the lawn.

I pace unfamiliar streets now
attempting new solutions
                to old problems
and the answers seldom come.

But there was a time
in the fall and winter
                of the year
when the sun's bright yellow
        mingled with the fog
and Kearny Street
                in San Francisco
was the whole world.

Sometimes I'm sorry
for love once known
it doesn't justify the years
you spend remembering.
I was always timid
about your loving me anyway
knowing the eagle
        does not hunt flies
and that worlds were larger
            than our love.

But I am happy still
that even for a moment
you laughed in my direction
and chased my nakedness
          down a lonely beach.

Maybe six months of love
is worth the lifetime
              you spend looking,
and marmalade and oysters
for breakfast one morning
and knowing you tried to love me
                              is enough.

For love is only moments
                here and there
it comes and goes quietly I think.
You hear it like silver bells
tied about the throats of cats
                now near—
now sounding far away.

I was loved on Kearny Street.
But no more the young heart
leaping in the dark room.

Vocal Lessons

You want to sing.
I could make it so.
But would you
          sing for me?

Not for my ears only,
but for my dissemination
to this world
and all the others,
but only after every note
was hummed and honed
to perfect pitch.

Each cadenza
ascended like a staircase,
me watching all those notes
forming in your chest
heaving upward
like a too-long suppressed sigh
until they reached
            and finally escaped
your so loved mouth.

Oh I could be a teacher
better than the best.
I'd have you singing
with your arms and legs
and all your body.
Your back no less
            than your full voice.

Every sparrow,
once he's learned
          to serenade,
leaves the nest
and soars out on his own
                    to fly.

I ask no security,
no contract from you,
only that you let me
give to you
          another life.

Using just
the raw ingredients
of your sweet voice,
and a little time,
I'd have you singing
softer than the mother hen
                    at mealtime
louder than the radio
        inside the wall.

Hopefully long after
you had flown your cage
some trust in me
would still remain.
Even if the need was gone
I'd take my chances
      on the trust.

Did I read
in small print somewhere
in brief but pointed
            program notes
that you want to sing?

I accept the challenge.
When do we begin?

The Weight of Winter Rain

The fireflies gone now
the trees low bending
with the weight of
    winter rain
I listen for the sound
       of winters past.
The years I walked
the rainy street
and filtered through
       the parks
in search of music people.
Creeping home to bed alone
to be with imaginary lovers
and hear the sound of Eden
ringing in my young ears.

I could go back
to San Francisco
if I still had
muscled thighs.
The trouble is
I run a little faster now.

What Common Language

No speeches have been
            written for us
and so we never speak.
But still they move
in front of me.
Unmet. Detached.
What common language
                could we know
    I wonder.
What words
of sensibility are left?

Old hellos and salutations
now snap back through jaws
as easily as they jumped out.

Conversation
   if it lives somewhere,
must be bitten off
        in Braille
or spoken in a code
but never passed
from hand to hand.

Do I sound as though
I've been out
seeking love again?
I have.
          But more.
I've seen it everywhere
and I go on seeing it.
In unmarked cars
as well as underneath
the well-worn badge.
In faces not lit up
          by firelight
but glowing
from the inside out.

I ache so much from love
I've seen but not yet shared
that I groan inside
not from periodic hunger
but from habit.

Breathing
other than my own
can now make any room
as painful
as unanswered prayers
                    must be
for those to whom religion
is the chord of life.

Once or twice
a face comes near,
and I look up
      and then look down.

New Year's Day

All in all
the year's been hard
and I'm lately tired.

Am I worthy, God?
Has this penance
day by day
made me deserving
or do I face another year
with no return
    on my investment?

How many Our Fathers
and cycles of Hail Marys
will bring Love out of loving?

Cycle

Only lonely men
know freedom.
Love,
as lovely as it is,
still ensnares.

Is it better then
to be on the outside
in the dark and free,
or caged contentedly
but still looking
out beyond the bars?

Tomorrow/1963

I know that love
is running in the snow.
I cannot see it but it's there.
As sure as caterpillars
     tunnel in the leaves
and winter weight
     bogs down the trees.

And so I search the highways
        and the hills.

There was a time
when bar talk
          and Bartok
did the job
and I would hurry home—
a stranger in my arms
or in my thoughts
to be content
and even comfortable
with San Francisco rain.

You'd be surprised
  the way the dripping rain
        from rooftops
can ease a man
     from out himself
      and into sun.

We're all older now,
losing this past year
Piaf's smile,
        Kennedy's promises
and Cocteau's jokes
                on everyone
(he said the ship
was going down, remember).

The year turns home.
Maybe tomorrow.

The Art of Catching Trains

1.
I came through
the clothesline maze
            of childhood
in basketball shoes.
Up from the cracked cement
            of sidewalks.
Long hair blowing in the breeze
from barber-college haircuts,
I moved into the country
knowing love better
        than long division.

Tricking out with women
                 twice my age
we acted out
our own French postcards.
Dr. Jekyll in the schoolyard.
Mr. Hyde behind the barn.

After school the trains,
their whistles known by heart.
Pennies flattened on a rail
and dresser drawers
        with matchbooks
            from every northern town,
thrown by unknown travelers
who never waved back.

I knew the U.P. right of way
                    so well
that gandy danders
              called me towhead
till they learned my name
and engineers would sometimes
whistle down the scale
              on seeing my arm raised.

Baseball's just a sissy game
to anyone who's waved
                    at passing trains.

You learn from hobos
the art of catching trains.
Locomotives slow at trestles
and whistle stops
            to hook the mail.

Diving through an open boxcar
you lie there
till your breath comes back.
Then standing in the doorway
            you're the king
as crowns of hills
            and towns go by
and nighttime
eats the summer up
and spits the stars
            across the sky.

How did I come to know
so many lonesome cities
with only pennies
            in my pockets?
I smiled a lot
and rode a lot of trains
and got to know conductors
and railroad bulls by name.
From Alamo to Naples is a ride
that took me nearly
            twenty years.
But here I am,
my cardboard suitcase
traded in for leather.

2.
Now a traveler
under the gray-black
                winter sky
moving down the mountain
        by torchlight,
I've come to find
a gathering of eagles.
Not for the sake of mingling
        with the great birds,
but only to justify
a thousand streets
                walked end to end.
Ten thousand evenings spent
listening to the small sounds
                        of the night
in station after station.

Not every town
in Switzerland
has a golden *Gondelbahn*,
but there are other ways
to climb the hills and reach
the lonesome cities of the world.

Riding friendly bodies
you can inch your way
         to Heaven
let alone the far side
         of the room.

And who'd deny
that brushing elbows
in certain streets
has not produced
          for every man
at least one vision
          of Atlantis.

For me old habits
don't break easily
I wait for trains.

Sometimes
I feel I've always been
just passing through.
On my way away, or toward.
Shouting alleluias
             in an unseen choir
or whispering *fados*
             down beneath my breath
      waiting for an echo
not an answer.
Everybody has the answers
or they'll make them up
                    for you.

Just once I'd like to hear
a brand-new question.

What about the trains
                 you ride
do they go fast or slow
would I recognize your face
clacking past the
                 poplar trees
if I were stationed
                 on some hill?

If I did I'd know you
by the look of nothing
                 in your eyes
the kindred look
             that travelers have
the one that says
             a tentative hello.

If while riding down the rails
you see a boy in overalls
along the railroad right-of-way
              wave as you go by.
Signal with a frown
you too are going down
          that same road.

Small boys need encouragement
the freight trains in their minds
will only take them just so far.
Be kind
    for small boys need to grow.

for Joyce Haber

Instructions to the Innocent

Initial Instructions

Go easy. No one will believe you if you come in fast. Take no one unaware. Give each new friend, potential enemy, or love time to do their own mind-making and deciding. And for as long as possible, be open with your own decisions. Never consciously run back home with more than you receive.

Be gentle. God, how all of us want and need that now. Don't cry out. I was only testing you, trying to be sure. Not of you, of me.

Eighteen

The moonrise
and the sunfall
are visible
to any blind man
with eyes enough
to feel the outline
of another blind man's
        breath.

Sunday: Two

I wish for you
Sweet Sunday psalms
and carols of an evening,
sung out clear and strong,
coming up from chests
you haven't been against
                just yet—
but will.

I wish you free,
face down in every lap
that walked away
without your head
pressed hard against
its Venus mound or crotch.

Surprising you
midsentence unsuspectingly
caring and carrying you
carefully to his own—
your own Eden.

I wish you
        vintage wine
in every Coca-Cola
                glass
an end to wishing
            signaling
you've found forever
at the end of now.

Could I command your mouth
to talk at my ear only
and climb on my mouth
                every time,
you know I would and more.

I'd wish beyond all reason.
Because I want
        beyond all want
                for you.

I would wish for you
                    the world
if it were good enough.

Each morning sky
hanging out there
clear as crystal
I'd reel in for you
and doing so, make real.

Though I have yet
to see a sky
or any world
quite good enough for you,
I keep on looking
as I keep a lookout still
                    for you.

Conversion

Jesus freak
pointing out each plane
of pain and pleasure.
I'm ready for
your fifty-mile-an-hour
            conversion.
Especially when your eyes
            perform baptism
and every smile you make
is some new sermon
served and said
without a speech or sentence.

Later when
the late show's gone
and only stars
light up the night
we'll celebrate communion
face to face
without wafers
   and no wine.

I'll give you all
and take back
   any excess
that you do not need.

Jesus freak
the name fits well.
And how the hounds of hell
must quake tonight.

Count me as a Christian
        from the time
our shoulders brushed
and both of us
stood sure and steady
knowing that the living church
entered into both of us
a minute from the time we met
or better still
            a minute less.

I am a saver
a holder-back,
but being you,
you'll have access
to it all.
The choice is yours.

And I'll accept your savior
your Jesus old or new
and you'll consent
to save me from myself.

Lesson: One

I leave you on the bed
still within the dark
        genuinely sorry
          that it came to this.
Then the long walk home
climbing the stairs
to be alone
        and maybe sleep,
    or whatever,
but not to think.

The year twenty gone
I concentrate on twenty-one
and so begin to wonder
              when it is
a man becomes a man.
Will I be officially informed
by the tax man
        or the rule-book maker?

I've noticed that the hair
upon my belly's darkened
and it moves toward my chest,
yet though a forest stands
where only trees once stood
              I don't feel different.

I leave you
          walk away
sorry for the first time.

Tomorrow when you waken
there'll be sun
and you'll forget.
But me,
think how it is for me
not knowing what
the transformation means
or if it's come or will come.

I leave you silent in the dark
but I know darkness too.

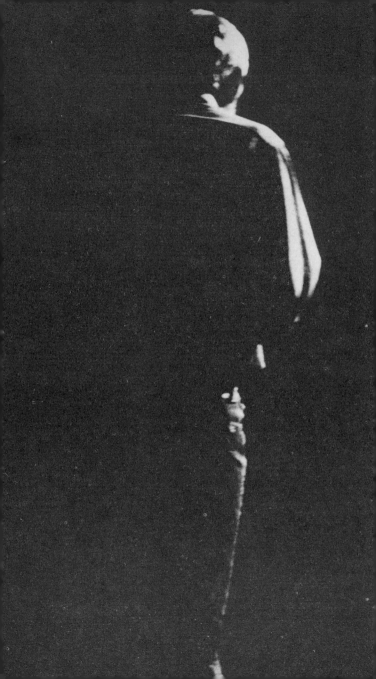

July 14

I wrote Paul this morning
after reading his poem,
        I told him,
it's ok to drop your pants
to old men sometimes
but I wouldn't recommend it
    as a way of life.

I didn't mail the letter.

We're all falling
we never learn about it
       till we land.

Paul might fall a different way
but who's to say which way is better
            till they've been there
    and come back safe.

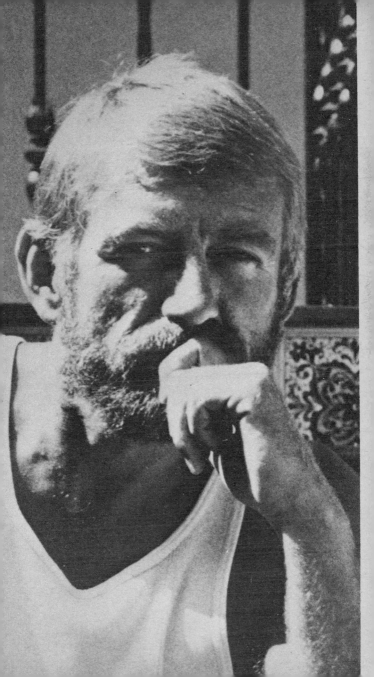

Living with Darkness

I can be happy
in the dark.
I can live with it.
I can turn once,
          twice,
     three times around
in the dark
before my eyes become
adjusted to the blackness
and not be frightened
                anymore.

Frightened,
I can be elated
at being left alone
when the alternative
is being with just anyone.

Private Spencer

Private Spencer
has a problem
his eyes are lonelier
        than most.

I saw a woman
follow him
halfway home once
failing to understand
until long after
     his wide footsteps
         had quickened
that that wasn't
what he wanted
       at all.

Scrub Pines
for Lowell Haver

Scrub pines struggle
through the underbrush,
sideways, d
      o
        w
          n,
then up again.
Never really heading skyward
they seem happy to survive
if not to really thrive.

Nature never helps
the scrub pine tree
it seems to caution
get there on your own,
wherever *there* is.
I'm not sure
that even that slow-growing,
stunted, slanted scrub
could tell you
where it's heading
and which branch
          leads the way.

Scrub pines finally
find their way.
Proud, predictably
             unpredictable
they shoot up through
the underbrush
             and underbelly
of long grass
in their own good time.

Try to help.
Clean and water down
          the root,
spread love
to the farthest limb.
It doesn't work.
Their resilience lies
in their own ability
to go and grow alone.

Straighten out
a scrub pine tree
and watch it
snap back in your face
even on a path
you thought familiar
and without peril.

I tried.
But the island,
let alone the world,
is full of stinging faces
        each of whom
        can make that statement.

        It might have been
                almost enough
if you'd have let me
watch you turn and grow
in your own way
at your own speed.
Even if I'd done my watching
        from an acre off.

But islands never reappear
in quite the same way
that you saw them first.
I couldn't find my way
to inlet or to island
            without direction
and certainly
you'd never lead me.

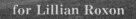

for Lillian Roxon

Death...
As a Beginning

To Begin With . . .

To begin with, every page is blank, until a word, a smudge, a paragraph is set down upon it. Some pages still stay blank after the most intricate, indelible story has been started.

The starting of a new story is always easy; it's the ending that comes hard. Knowing when to draw conclusions, the point to let your characters stop leading you so that you can take command. When is the sum enough to provide the summing up?

I do not know how death will come to me, though once I thought I did. How I will greet it will depend on how hard or easy it comes in. I am very sure that any pain that might accompany my going could not be as bad or worse than some I've known within my life. I am resolved that, if I can, I will view the end as the writer does the blank page just in front of him, a beginning.

Butterfly

Yesterday
a butterfly
flew through the eaves
of Villa Trenta
and came to land
upon the middle of my arm.

He crawled with sureness
down to my hand
then back along my shoulder.
He fluttered there
a moment only
then fell dead,
a victim of the heat
or something higher up.

If God
can strike down
birds and butterflies
and then change rain
                to rainbows
and clouds to grays and whites
of every hue,
then the ugliness
        I've shown of late
has surely marked me
for an early death.

What troubles me
            is not
my disappearance
but my lack of being
troubled by it.
I am willful now
toward well-meaning friends
when I should have will instead
to fight off that oncoming end.

Bar Forty-six

I know
I'm coming to the coda
as I know all waltzes stop.

If we stay at distance
five years more is all I need
If you hold me
fifteen minutes should be plenty.

Pieces of Glass

Can the living
reach the dead?
Yes, I said,
as I lay dying.
And if they can't,
I heard
the unknown say,
it's not from
any lack of trying.

Exercise

Lingering
as the dying do
between that life just past
and the still unknown,
I only know enough
about myself as yet
          to know
that I don't know enough.

Nor can I say
I know what's missing—
voids are voids
and only seen completely
after we've had victories
                    over them.

Freedom

Free I am.
I have no bills to pay.
My debts are squared,
the edges smoothed out
                    perfectly.
My *ducks are in a row*
        and I can sail.

There are borders
in this final life
that were not here
        at nineteen
or at twenty-three.
I'll not admit
that I erected them
or even that I helped.

What if I did
not even knowing
what I built
with my erector set?
I am not accountable.

My newfound freedom
only came just now
and I'm experimenting
        with it still.

Happily there's no one left
                    to disappoint
if I should stumble
          in the dark
or die while diving
through a dream
that didn't end.

To those who'd jail me
let them try.
My boundaries
          and responsibilities,
if they were ever there,
now blur into a single
tie-dyed day.

Flying in the Face of God

In a biplane once
flying higher
than I thought I could
I half expected
that beyond each cloud
      God waited
with the face
    of Father Christmas
or the frown of some
      proud farmer
who resented someone
       climbing up
   his private hill.

We didn't meet.
But that is not to say
we didn't touch
        or pass by close.

Since that day
I've felt the need
to one time fly
beyond and still beyond—
up to where the air's
            so thin
that only God
    could live there
        with security,
if I do and when I do
as I fall back to earth
I'll know that I've been
pushed or nudged by a hand
     of sure direction.

Orly Field
for Doug Davis

I often wonder
why you ran so fast,
if it was all to end
that day at Orly Field.
You might have stopped
          in Spain awhile
and let the sun
go singing in your head.
Or walked the hills in Hydra.
Or even stayed at home.
Atlanta's not that bad
          in summertime.

You might have listened
                for the wind
and got to know it better.
They say it comes in handy
                    later on.
I might have been
        a better friend
if I hadn't trusted time.

If the dead can hear
                the living
raise your head a little
and I'll try to show you
                    Spain.

One Day I'll Follow the Birds

One day I'll follow the birds
disappearing into the rain
going in a hurry, then gone,
glad to be in flight again
not sure why I'm running.

There are some wounds
I never speak about.
Some things that words
have done to me
that none will ever know.

But one gray day
I'll follow a funeral
          out of town
on the heels of the birds
disappearing into the rain.

for Adela Rogers St. Johns

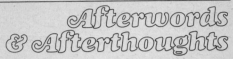

Afterwords & Afterthoughts

Afterwords & Afterthoughts

When it's over, love, someone's birthday, the big game or the funeral, words not only come to mind that would have been said earlier if the brain was always working, but recriminations and prayers for replay fill the mind and work it overtime. A conversation in the head long after every chance has passed is not unusual, more the rule.

After every loss, or what we term to be our losses, a hundred master plans are planned, a dozen avenues we might have taken, had not a certain road been blocked, stretch out before us like a city map.

Finally the afterthoughts afterward are lost like all the melodies that had no meaning and the memories that did.

Afterthought, One

Now the memory blurs.
You didn't feed it.
Not to worry,
not to worry.
I'll keep filling in
the holes until they're whole.

Afterthought, Two

Come then strangers
and those of you I know,
form as one.
I fear you've done so
anyway and already.

And if your name
be litany or lie
I'll love you all the same
if you'll come close enough
        to let me.

Monochrome

A black kite
flying in the distance
further down the beach
        then gone.
Black birds too are here
scavenging fish heads,
chasing off the killdeer
        and the gull.

The sea—
not blue but double grays,
goes on about its business.
It seems calmer now,
quieter today.

How long will it take,
another century perhaps
till every cloud above
                    the water
hangs there hidden, black.

The sand.
I give it fifty years.
The stars, already dimming,
                    fifty more.
Blackness in the end
will overtake them both.

How is it
people fear the dark?
Not me, I'm reconciled.
As every day I see
        the blackness grow,
I've come to terms with it,
it knows I know.

Yet I wonder
if the darkness
ever hungers
      or grows lonely
for the light
it's left behind.

The final blackness
after all is death.
That's what the elements
are moving to,
I doubt they have regrets.

No cards are being played
no hands dealt out
determining exactly when.
A single game
        of solitaire perhaps
and when it ends
it starts again.

Where the Big Boys Play

One day a man will take you
      on the high roads;
After a time
    he'll leave you
   someplace nice
or tell you where
the big boys play.
They usually string out
       their games
   in someone's shadow.
 It could be yours.
More likely mine,
for mine's grown longer
and there's more room here.

I ache to learn
some new games now,
I've been away
from town too long.
To see a new door open
I'd go almost anywhere.
Even backward,
if I thought
         I had the time.

I'm mad at midnight
for the things
         it didn't do,
that doesn't mean
I wouldn't take
a chance again.

Few angels
have been heard to sing
but many purr
when stroked just so.

Lie down and leave
your imprint in the sand,
my hand will trace it
into everything I need.
That's how reality begins,
shadows made something real
or reality turned back into a
                    shadow.

I need the sureness
of the shadow world again.
To make me whole.

If I am anything at all
I'm what I've gotten
            out of sand.
Not only that washed in
      from seas and islands
but any piece of earth
      (however small)
a man can hold
securely in his hand.

Catch me in the sunlight.
Catch me pacing
              past the trees.
Build a fence around me
the moment that you
              see me running.
I'm so elusive sometimes
I miss the things
worth stopping for.

I need.
Not more trees.
Not more rain
in backyard barrels
or racing down the gutters
              to the drain.

I need the comfort
of a friendly back or belly.
Seen sometimes in magazines
or made up in my mind.

You know the ones I mean.
They shout out at you
like the trees in April.
Or blossom on you
like strawberry smiles.

I have been assaulted
by soft smiles
        at a distance.
The way some radios
                attack you
from across the room
when you're strapped up
        in a barber chair.
The way you're raped
by Muzak in an elevator.

Now comes the time
for closeness once again.
Turn me over gently.
Hold me for the man I am.
Smooth out the wrinkles
                on my face
And love me—please.
Because I need.

The big boys play
in someone's shadow
            down the street
and I'm detached.

That's as it should be,
for I need more than games.

Take a chance on me.
I haven't any name
but what you'll give me
                when you leave.

Fiore/1812

If I could
set down eighteen lines
upon a clean white page
that so expressed you
detailed in minute
and grand detail
the sockets of your
        deep brown eyes,
the girth of you
omitting not one millennium
                of your size,
if I could tell
exactly what it's like
to climb through you
and into myself
then back inside/outside
        you again,

if I could say
face to face to you
in rhyme
    or out of rhythm
how I feel this day
after only one night's
reading of you,
say it straight
for your ears only
yet with no complexity
so that everyone
        would understand
then I could write
my final poem
    and be done.

I could
turn the page
and find but one line
          not twelve
one single sentence
that summed it up,
here it is I'd say
          all for you.
Everything I've made
          from my life
and with my life
here it is—
All I've done
down nearly forty years
from crying in the cradle
to sobbing in the spotlight,
every laugh and long sigh
                    in between
was but a preparation for just now.

Could I say it
well enough
    to be believed by you,
I'd run home to Pine Street
and open all the windows
                    W I D E
and shout to all the neighbors
look who's living here inside
                we are
surrounded by a greener green
than any meadow ever knew
and a multi-colored bed
wide as any known or unknown sea.

Fiore!
I would shout aloud
flower of a different hue.
Fiore with a mind
of so many unseen colors
that the dahlia
            or the tie-dyed rose
would never dare compete with you.

If I could set down
  eighteen lines
on the virgin page
followed by a second twelve
to some a statement
   of us up,
I'd dwell on every possibility
leaving out the humps
    and hurdles.
  No impossibilities exist
to keep from bringing
   each of us
into the realm of one.

Come into me
as I've lately come
   inside of you.
A fusion we are.
The best of both
that's made when we're together
   a third.

The First

No matter when I start
that first day's walk
along the tide's white ragged edge,
someone's been ahead of me.

I went at noon the first day,
        ten the next.
Finally at sunrise
I started out
and on this very morning
I was up before the sun
guided by the whitecaps only
luminous in the dimming starlight.

When at last the light
began to rim the far horizon
I saw beside my own, new footprints
in the Monday sand
a larger imprint trailing on
                ahead of me.
And beside that wide stride
on this quiet beach
the soft impression of a dog
who must have trotted
by his master's side.

I've but one more morning
left to me
before I trade Très Vidas
             for the city,
but if I have to start out
down the beach at midnight
                or before
I'm determined to confront
that brown beach man
who dares to think
he loves my ocean
more than me.

And anyway,
the ocean's all
that I have left.
There won't be anyone again,
but there will always be
sea water and sea things
to wash the memories
            into one another.

That's a comfort
not to be taken lightly,
considering the sea
            is all I have.

About the Author

ROD McKUEN was born in Oakland, California, and has traveled extensively throughout the world both as a concert artist and a writer. In just over six years seven of his books of poetry have sold in excess of ten million copies in hardcover, making him the best-selling and most widely read poet of all times. In addition he is the best-selling living author writing in any hardcover medium today. His poetry is taught and studied in schools, colleges, universities and seminaries throughout the world, and the author spends a good deal of his time visiting and lecturing on campus.

Mr. McKuen is the composer of more than fifteen hundred songs that have been translated into Spanish, French, Dutch, German, Russian, Japanese, Czechoslovakian, Chinese, Norwegian and Italian, among other languages. They account for the sale of more than one hundred fifty million records.

His film music has twice been nominated for Motion Picture Academy Awards. Rod McKuen's classical music, including symphonies, concertos, piano sonatas and his very popular *Adagio for Harp & Strings*, is performed by leading orchestras in the United States and throughout Europe. In May, 1972, the Royal Philharmonic Orchestra in London premiered his *Concerto #3 for Piano & Orchestra*, and an orchestral suite, *The Plains of My Country*. In

1973, the Louisville Orchestra commissioned Mr. McKuen to compose a suite for orchestra and narrator, entitled *The City*. It was premiered in Louisville and Danville, Kentucky, in October, 1973, and was subsequently nominated for a Pulitzer Prize in music.

Among his newest commissions is a multi-media ballet requested by Nicolas Petrov, director of the Pittsburgh Ballet, to commemorate the American Bicentennial. It will have its premiere in that city in 1976. His *Symphony #3,* commissioned by the Menninger Foundation in honor of their fiftieth anniversary, has just been premiered in Topeka, Kansas.

Before becoming a best-selling author and composer, Mr. McKuen worked as a laborer, radio disc jockey and newspaper columnist.

The author spent two years in the army, during and after the Korean War.

Rod McKuen makes his home in California in a rambling Spanish house, which he shares with a menagerie of Old English sheep dogs and a dozen cats. He likes outdoor sports, driving, and has recently started taking flying lessons.

He is currently working on a lengthy book of prose about America and has recently completed a very atypical book of prose-poetry entitled *Beyond the Boardwalk*, published by Cheval Books. *Beyond the Boardwalk* was started several years ago and put aside every time new projects came up. The author termed the finished work as "self-indulgent."

If you've enjoyed this book so far, we think you might enjoy every bit as much a new publication entitled INSIDE STANYAN. Published 5 times a year, INSIDE STANYAN is more than a magazine about a record company, it's a publication that currently is offering an authoritative biography of Rod McKuen in installments, news of the recording and book world, contests, special offers for free records, and rock bottom prices for recordings by such great artists as Judy Garland, Cleo Laine, Mabel Mercer, Carmen McRae, Eartha Kitt, Dinah Shore, Alice Faye, Jacques Brel, many previously unavailable film soundtracks and the best of Broadway, London, and Hollywood . . . and more than 3 dozen albums and half a dozen books by Rod McKuen.

INSIDE STANYAN is not like any other publication. There are bright, amusing columns, glimpses into the life of the entertainment industry, and most important—if you're a Rod McKuen fan and we assume you are if you're reading this book—news on Rod's upcoming concerts, recordings, and day to day life.

For $10, you will receive not only the 5 issues of INSIDE STANYAN, but as a bonus, any one of any of the five records listed below (a $6.98 value *if* they were available anywhere else, but they are not available anywhere else—not even your local record store).

THIS IS NOT A BOOK OR RECORD CLUB

You do not receive unwanted merchandise, dated announcements, and you are under no obligation whatsoever . . . other than to receive 5 copies of INSIDE STANYAN throughout the year and to listen to and enjoy for as long as records last, the album you've chosen. INISIDE STANYAN will keep you abreast of all the new Stanyan releases, what's going on with other record companies and book publishers, and provide the kind of glimpse into what makes McKuen tick that nobody else has been able to come up with. Also a portion of your subscription money goes to benefit Animal Concern.

Sources

"The Spectator," "Video Tape," "Winter Night," "High Heavens There Are," "Vocal Lessons," "Living with Darkness," "Butterfly," "Monochrome," "Encounters," "Solitaire," "To Begin With . . . ," "Afterwords & Afterthoughts," and the other prose, including the author's foreword, are published here for the first time.

"Room," "Advance/Retreat," "Supper," "Fiore/1812" and "Scrub Pines" are from *Rusting in the Rain,* to be published by Simon and Schuster in September, 1975.

"Sheridan Square, '74/A Diary in Miniature" will be the basis for a new book.

"Night" is from the private printing of *A Man Alone*.

"Closet," "Soldier, One/Tagu, Korea—1955," "Oval Window," "Private Spencer," and "Conversion" are from *Beyond the Boardwalk*.

"While Drifting," "The Need" ("Thirty-six"), "The Weight of Winter Rain" ("Twenty-seven"), and "One Day I'll Follow the Birds" are from *Listen to the Warm*.

"Journeymen," "April 12," "Shadows and

Safety," "July 14," and "Where the Big Boys Play" ("Prologue") are from *In Someone's Shadow*.

"Eighteen" and "Bar Forty-six" ("Twenty-four") are from *Caught in the Quiet*.

"Holidays," "Jimjann," "State Beach," "Poem," "Day Song," "Night Song," "Poem, 2," and "Orly Field" are from *Stanyan Street & Other Sorrows*. "Poem, 2" ("I Have No Special Bed") first appeared on the album *Time of Desire*.

"New Year's Day" is from *The Carols of Christmas*.

"Tomorrow/1963" is from *Twelve Years of Christmas*.

"School" and "Cycle" are from *With Love*.

"The Hermit Crab," "April Man," "Lesson: One," "Lesson: Two," and "Freedom" are from *And to Each Season*.

"Sunday: Two" and "Flying in the Face of God" are from *Come to Me in Silence*.

"Hotel Room," "Concerto for Four Hands," "Paris," and "The Art of Catching Trains" are from *Lonesome Cities*.

"Oakland Bus Depot/1951" ("December 10") and "August 31" are from *And Autumn Came*.

"The Dandelion" ("Afterwards") and "What Common Language" ("Closer Watch") are from *Fields of Wonder*.

"On the Way to Sacramento" and "Pieces of Glass" appeared in the European edition of *Moment to Moment*. They also appeared in the 1974 domestic edition, as did "Tuesday Afternoon," "Thursday Evening," "The First," and "Exercise" ("Prelude: The Leaving").

"I Roll Better with the Night" is from *The Seasons*.

"Those Who Found the Time" ("Lilacs") is from the *Animal Concern Calendar* (*1972 Rod Mc-Kuen Calendar & Datebook*). "Winter Night" ("Night Climb") and "Afterthought, Two" are also from the *Animal Concern Calendar* (*1974 Rod McKuen Calendar & Datebook*).

"Afterthought, One" appeared in *Folio* and the British edition of *Caught in the Quiet*.

Index to First Lines

Recent Recordings by Rod McKuen

SLEEP WARM   Stanyan
GOOD-TIME MUSIC   Stanyan/Warner Bros.
CENTENNIAL   Stanyan
BEYOND THE BOARDWALK   Stanyan
ALONE   Stanyan/Warner Bros.
SEASONS IN THE SUN   Warner Bros.
BACK TO CARNEGIE HALL   Warner Bros.
LOVE SONGS   Stanyan
AFTER MIDNIGHT   Stanyan
THE CITY
   (Suite for Orchestra &
      Narrator)   Louisville Records
THE PLAINS OF MY COUNTRY   Stanyan
LIVE AT THE SYDNEY OPERA
      HOUSE   Stanyan
GREATEST HITS VOL. 4   Warner Bros.

For a complete catalogue of Rod McKuen's books and records, write: Stanyan Records, 8440 Santa Monica Boulevard, Los Angeles, California 90069.